SQL Server Fundamentals for the Accidental DBA

Eric Johnson

✦ Addison-Wesley

Upper Saddle River, NJ • Boston • Indianapolis • San Francisco

New York • Toronto • Montreal • London • Munich • Paris • Madrid

Cape Town • Sydney • Tokyo • Singapore • Mexico City

Many of the designations used by manufacturers and sellers to distinguish their products are claimed as trademarks. Where those designations appear in this book, and the publisher was aware of a trademark claim, the designations have been printed with initial capital letters or in all capitals.

The author and publisher have taken care in the preparation of this book, but make no expressed or implied warranty of any kind and assume no responsibility for errors or omissions. No liability is assumed for incidental or consequential damages in connection with or arising out of the use of the information or programs contained herein.

The publisher offers excellent discounts on this book when ordered in quantity for bulk purchases or special sales, which may include electronic versions and/or custom covers and content particular to your business, training goals, marketing focus, and branding interests. For more information, please contact:

U.S. Corporate and Government Sales
(800) 382-3419
corpsales@pearsontechgroup.com

For sales outside the United States please contact:

International Sales
international@pearson.com

Visit us on the Web: informit.com/aw

Copyright © 2009 Pearson Education, Inc.

ISBN-13: 978-0-321-60277-0
ISBN-10: 0-321-60277-3
Text printed in the United States on recycled paper at R. R. Donnelley in Crawfordsville, Indiana.
First printing January 2009

Editor-in-Chief
Karen Gettman

Acquisitions Editor
Joan Murray

Managing Editor
Patrick Kanouse

Project Editor
Jennifer Gallant

Copy Editor
San Dee Phillips

Proofreader
Paula Lowell

Publishing Coordinator
Olivia Basegio

Contents

Preface

Introduction

I have worked with SQL Server for many years and in that time, I have worked with many different individuals from developers, to system administrators, to data architects. One thing I have noticed is that while SQL Server has sprung up all over the place, there is not always an experienced database administrator looking after them. Client applications will install free versions of SQL Server, known previously as the Microsoft SQL Server Desktop Engine or MSDE and more recently as SQL Server Express Edition. These free versions have many of the same care and feeding requirements as full-blown copies of SQL Server, but often they are left to their own devices. In addition, I have worked with many developers over the years who are fantastic at their jobs and know how to write applications, but they sometime falter when it comes to understanding database structure and design methodologies. It is for these system administrators and developers, these accidental DBAs that I did this LiveLesson series.

What Is This LiveLesson About?

In this LiveLesson, I have tried to take my experience and knowledge of SQL Server and database design and put it into an easy to follow series of lesson to help you understand the fundamentals of administer SQL Server. By no means is this course meant to cover everything about the product or even cover every aspect of the topics discussed. My goal is to provide you with a foundation of knowledge about SQL Server so that you can properly manage it or work with it as a developer.

Deciding what to put in this LiveLesson was a challenging task. Often it came down to a simple question, would a company need to hire a full-time DBA if they where to use a particular feature? Where the answer was yes, I choose not to cover the feature. For example, managing SQL Server replication can be a daunting task and probably not one to be undertaken by an accidental DBA. What you will find in the LiveLesson is everything you will need to know in order to manage SQL Server enough to keep it backed up, secure, and running.

Who Should Use This Course?

Anyone who has found that he or she must manage or work with some version of SQL Server when his or her primary job function does not include such tasks will find this course useful. Windows administrators who find SQL Server behind SMS or Sharepoint or .NET developers who are told to write an application that uses SQL Server as a back-end data store should have a working knowledge of SQL Server and that is what this course provides.

How This Course Is Organized

The course is structured around the basic task that one may find himself needing to perform on a SQL Server. Some lessons will build on knowledge gained in an earlier lesson but in general each lesson covers a very specific topic and you can skip around if you find one area more important than another. The LiveLesson format makes it perfect for you to cover a subject and then come back a month later and view a different subject. The lessons and their content are described as follows.

1. SQL Server Overview

   This lesson aims to give you an overview of what SQL Server is and the different flavors of SQL Server you may encounter. We will also cover the different components of SQL Server that are included in the product.

2. Common Uses of SQL Server

   In order to manage all your SQL Servers, you first must find them. In this lesson, we will look at different places where you might find SQL Server in your environment. The goal is to provide you with more information about how SQL Server is used so that you can recognize situations where SQL Servers may be in use.

3. SQL Server Management Studio

   You will work with many tools in the process of managing SQL Servers, but none more so than the SQL Server Management Studio (SSMS). The goal of this lesson will be to orient you with SSMS and show you how it is used.

4. SQL Server Configuration Manager

   Continuing our look at tools, this lesson will introduce you to the Configuration Manager and how it is used to manage the settings of the various services.

5. SQL Server Profiler

   A fantastic tool for analysis and troubleshooting is the Profiler. In this brief introduction we will show you the basics of Profiler and make sure you know how to get around with the tool.

6. Business Intelligence Development Studio

   If you're developing database projects such as Integration Services packages or Reporting Services reports, you will use the Business Intelligence Development Studio (BIDS). This lesson will help you get familiar with the tool.

7. Understanding Tables

   This lesson serves as the first of two lessons that will cover relational database basics. It is easier to manage SQL Server if you have at least a passing understanding of what databases are and how they are structured. In this lesson, we will focus on the foundation of databases, namely tables.

8. Understanding Relationships

This lesson builds on the preceding by extending our discussion of relational databases. We will look at how the data in tables is joined through the concept of relationships.

9. Database Files

This lesson provides you with some detail as to how SQL Server manages databases. We will look at the different files that make up a database and how they are managed.

10. The Transaction Log

Crucial to the operation of SQL Server and therefore crucial to your knowledge is the transaction log. This lesson aims to explain the workings of the transaction log and to give you an idea of how recovery models affect its use.

11. Understanding System Databases

System database are used by SQL Server to keep all its internal processes up and running. We will look at each system database and how each contributes to the function of SQL Server as a whole.

12. Processor Settings

Often SQL Server is installed on a server with a few other applications running. In this lesson, we will look at the settings that control how SQL Server interacts with the server's CPUs.

13. Memory Settings

Just as important as the CPUs, memory also plays an enormous role for SQL Server. This lesson will show you the available memory settings and explain why you might need to make changes.

14. Backing Up Databases

A crucial task when working with SQL Server is backing up the databases. This lesson will show you what you need to know to make sure you can back up your databases and protect yourself from data loss.

15. Scheduling Backups

This lesson will be an introduction to SQL Server jobs. We will look specifically at how you can schedule routine maintenance such as backups in order to reduce the amount of manual work you need to put into managing SQL Server.

16. Restoring Databases

What good is backing up if you can't restore your database in the event of a loss? This lesson will provide you with the information necessary to perform a database restore.

17. Restoring System Databases

   Restoring System databases is a little different than restoring user databases. In this lesson we will look at those differences and walk through the process of restoring system databases.

18. Managing Logins

   Your first line of security is the login. This lesson will explain logins and show you how to create them and manage the permissions assigned to each login.

19. Managing Users

   Users are separate from logins and control the access granted into individual databases. In this lesson, we will look at what users are and how they are managed.

20. Database Roles

   Database roles are used to manage groups of users and assign the users permissions to do things in a database. This lesson aims to arm you with the information you need to manage database roles or even create your own.

21. Ownership Chaining

   This lesson will focus on a discussion of ownership chaining. This is an important concept in security and without fully understanding it, you may be handing out more permissions than your users need. We will talk specifically about what ownership changing is and look at some real-world examples.

22. Data Manipulation Language

   This will be the first lesson where we look at Transact SQL or T-SQL. T-SQL is the language used to work with SQL Server data and objects. In this lesson, we look at Data Manipulation Language (DML), which is used to work with the data being stored in your database.

23. Data Definition Language

   In order to create and modify objects in databases such as tables or views, you use Data Definition Language (DDL). In this lesson, we will look at the basics of DDL and how it is used.

24. Stored Procedures

   In addition to structures such as tables, databases are also made up of programming structures that allows you to run T-SQL code. The most common of these structures are stored procedures. In this lesson, we will look at what stored procedures are, how they are created, and how you set up security on them.

25. Functions

   This lesson will cover functions, another programming option in SQL Server databases.

26. Views

   This lesson will cover views. Views provide access to data without the need to access a table directly. We will look at what you need to know to use views effectively.

27. Triggers

   Triggers allow you to have bits of T-SQL run automatically in response to an event such as data being inserted into a table. This lesson will cover the different types of triggers and how you can use them in your databases.

28. CLR Integration

   With the release of SQL Server 2005, we were given the ability to used CLR code structures within SQL Server. This lesson will show you how this is accomplished and how you can make stored procedures, functions, or types in SQL Server that reference CLR code.

29. Indexing Overview

   Indexing is a huge topic in the world of SQL Server. This lesson will provide you with the basics of what indexes are and how SQL Server uses them to find data.

30. Working with Indexes

   This lesson will build on the last by providing you with what you need to know about the different types of indexes. In addition, we will look at how each type of index is implemented.

31. Included Columns

   This final indexing lesson will discuss a relatively new feature of SQL Server: included columns in indexes. We will look at what they are and how they are implemented in SQL Server.

32. Application Security

   We have looked at several security concepts and this lesson will bring these concepts together to help you make a real-world decision. We will look at the most common options for allowing applications access to SQL Server and the pros and cons of each.

33. Abstraction Layers

   This final lesson will be a discussion on creating abstraction layers. Abstraction layers have several uses and we will examine each as well as take a look at the problems that can arise when you don't have an abstraction layer.

Playing the DVD

If your Windows system is configured with AutoPlay on, the video will automatically start when you insert the DVD into your drive. However, if AutoPlay is off, you will need to insert the DVD into the drive, launch Windows Explorer, navigate to the root folder of the DVD, and double-click on the file called "Start_livelesson.exe."

This LiveLessons product is designed to run at a screen resolution of 1280 × 1024 or higher. Please adjust your screen resolution for the best playback experience.

LiveLessons DVD System Requirements

Operating system: Windows 98, 2000, XP, or Vista. Multimedia: DVD drive, 1024 × 768 or higher display, and sound card with speakers. Computer: 500MHz or higher, 128MB RAM or more.

About the Author

Eric S. Johnson, is the co-founder of Consortio Services and the primary Database Technologies Consultant; he is also a Microsoft SQL Server MVP. He has been recognized by Microsoft as an MVP for his expertise in SQL Server. His background in information technology is diverse, ranging from operating systems and hardware to specialized applications and development. He has even done his fair share of work on networks. Since IT is really just a way to support business processes, he also acquired his MBA in 2004. All in all, he has more than 10 years of experience with IT, a great amount of which has been working with Microsoft SQL Server. Eric has managed and designed databases of all shapes and sizes. He has delivered numerous SQL Server training classes and webcasts as well as presentations at national technology conferences. In addition, he is active in the local SQL Server community, serving as the president of the Colorado Springs SQL Server Users Group. He has published works from technical magazine articles for the likes of *Redmond Magazine* to authoring books such as *A Developer's Guide to Data Modeling for SQL Server,* published by Addison-Wesley.

lesson ⊙ 1

SQL Server Overview

What You Will Learn

SQL Server is Microsoft's Relational Database Management System (RDBMS). It consists of several components and the database engine. In this lesson, we define SQL Server and all its related components. We also look at all the available editions of SQL Server from the free Express edition to the do-everything Enterprise edition.

We Will Cover

- SQL Server product overview
- Components of SQL Server
- Editions of SQL Server

Notes from the Lesson

SQL Server consists of several components.

- Database Engine
- Reporting Services
- Integration Services
- Analysis Services

When selecting an edition of SQL Server, you have many different choices.

- Enterprise Edition
- Standard
- Workgroup
- Web

- Compact

- Express

- Developer

lesson ⊙ 2

Common Uses of SQL Server

What You Will Learn

SQL Server has come a long way from its humble beginnings, and you might even be surprised to learn all the different areas in which SQL Server is put to use. In this lesson, you look at some of the more common uses of SQL Server. Knowing where to look for SQL Server and how it is used will aid your understanding of the product as you get into some of the more meaty lessons.

We Will Cover

- Using SQL Server for custom applications

- Using SQL Server with third-party applications

- Using SQL Server as the backend for other Microsoft products

Notes from the Lesson

Use SQL Server in many different roles in an organization.

- **Custom Applications**—Use SQL Server as the backend to custom applications that organizations build in-house. These can be full-blown .NET applications or even PowerShell scripts.

- **Third-Party Applications**—Many third-party applications use SQL Server as their data store. This can include helpdesk applications, CRM Tools, Inventory Management, and more.

- **Backend to other Microsoft Applications**—Many Microsoft applications, such as SMS or SharePoint, use SQL Server to store data.

lesson ⊙ 3

SQL Server Management Studio

What You Will Learn

SQL Server Management Studio (SSMS), as shown in Figure 3.1, is the primary tool you use to administer and manage your SQL Server instances.

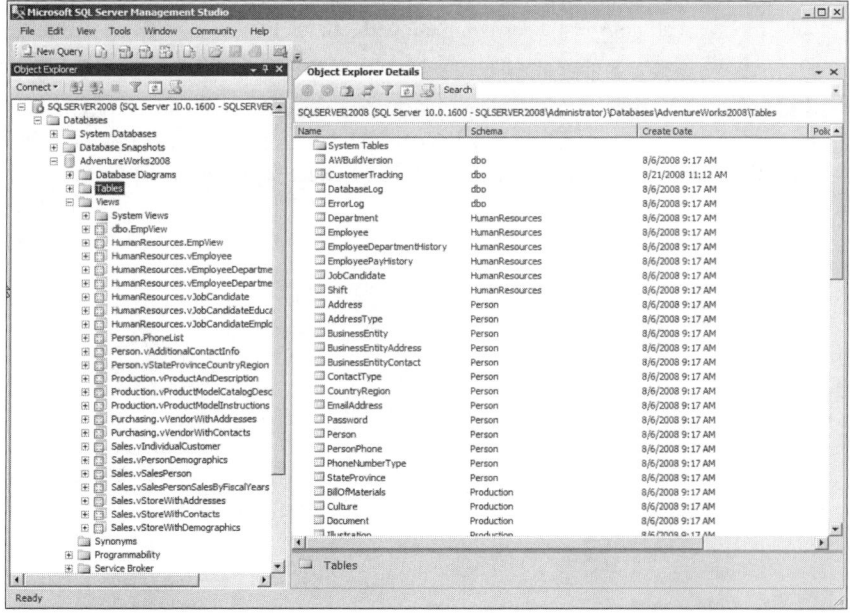

Figure 3.1   The SQL Server Management Studio.

The purpose of this lesson is to make sure that you are familiar with SQL Server Management Studio. This tool will be used a lot in the LiveLesson and in the real world, so understanding it is critical to your success.

We Will Cover

- Connecting to SQL Servers

- How database objects are organized into folders

- How to register SQL Servers

- How to run queries

- The differences in SQL Server Management Studio Express

Notes from the Lesson

- SQL Server Management Studio can be launched by clicking Start | All Programs | Microsoft SQL Server 2008 | SQL Server Management Studio.

- SSMS is, by default, broken into two halves. On the left is the Object Explorer pane and on the right is the Object Explorer Details pane.

- To make managing more than one SQL Server easier, you can use the Registered Servers toolbar to store all your instances complete with connection details. To open the Registered Servers toolbar, select View | Registered Servers or use the keyboard shortcut Ctrl+Alt+G.

- In addition to being a GUI for managing SQL Servers, SSMS allows you to run queries against servers. To open a new query window, click the New Query button in the toolbar or right-click a database in the Object Explorer and select New Query.

lesson ⊙ 4

SQL Server Configuration Manager

What You Will Learn

The SQL Server Configuration Manager, as shown in Figure 4.1, is the primary tool for making configuration changes to all the services that are a part of SQL Server.

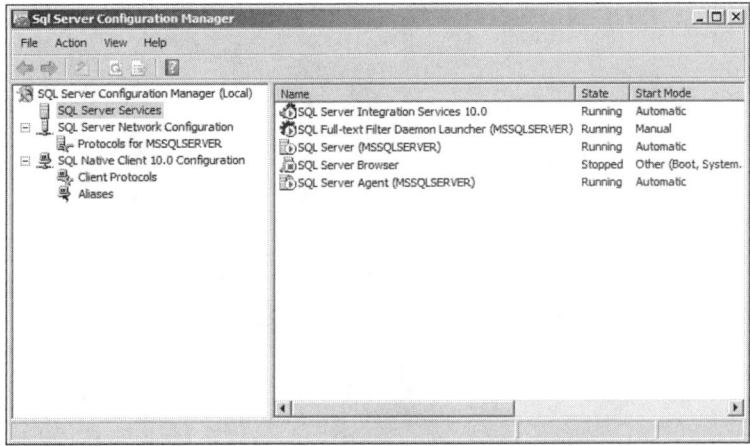

Figure 4.1   The SQL Server Configuration Manager.

This tool allows you to define many aspects of the services such as security credentials, start-up mode, ports, and start-up parameters. In addition, the SQL Server Configuration Manager allows you to set up the communication parameters so that a client can connect to a server.

We Will Cover

- Configuring SQL Server services
- Well-known ports for services

- Configuring server protocol
- Setting up the native client

Notes from the Lesson

- The first instance on SQL Server installed will run on port 1433.
- The default port for the SQL Server Browser service is 1434.
- Service start-up parameters are on the Advanced tab of the Service Properties dialog box. You can open the properties by right-clicking a service and selecting Properties.

lesson ⊙ 5

SQL Server Profiler

What You Will Learn

The SQL Server Profiler, as shown in Figure 5.1, traces activity on your SQL Servers.

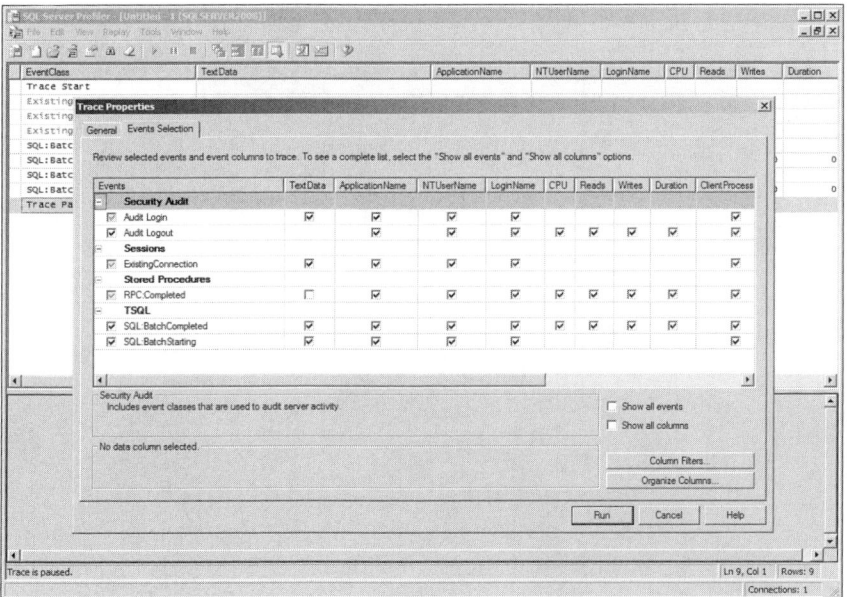

Figure 5.1   The SQL Server Profiler.

Use the data captured by Profiler to improve performance or troubleshoot problems on your servers. A lot of options are available for the types of events and data that Profiler can capture, so take some time to really dig around this tool and figure out everything it is capable of doing.

We Will Cover

- Setting up traces

- Trace results

- Adding events to traces

- Adding additional capture data to traces

Notes from the Lesson

- Launch SQL Server Profiler by clicking Start | All Programs | Microsoft SQL Server 2008 | Performance Tools | SQL Server Profiler.

- You can add events to Profiler to tell it what activity to watch for and further filter those events to specific captured data, such as a specific database.

- By selecting columns in trace properties, you can tell Profiler what data you want captured for specific events.

- Run Profiler from a machine other than your SQL Server. By tracing too much data, Profiler can have an impact on the SQL Server.

lesson ⊙ 6

Business Intelligence Development Studio

What You Will Learn

The SQL Server Business Intelligence Development Studio (BIDS), as shown in Figure 6.1, is a stripped-down version of Visual Studio that allows you to develop various SQL Server projects.

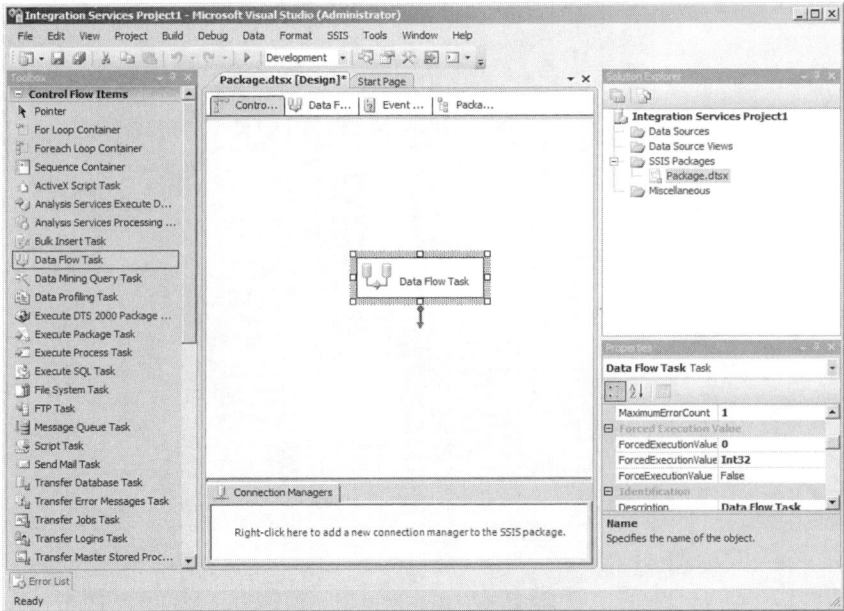

Figure 6.1   The SQL Server Business Intelligence Development Studio.

We Will Cover

- An overview of the Business Intelligence Development Studio

- Database project types

Notes from the Lesson

- Launch SQL Server BIDS by clicking Start | All Programs | Microsoft SQL Server 2008 | SQL Server Business Intelligence Development Studio.

- You can use BIDS to build several database projects including SSIS Packages. Reporting Server Reports, and Analysis Services projects.

- BIDS is a plug-in to Visual Studio. If you have Visual Studio installed, that is what will open when you launch BIDS.

lesson ▶ 7

Understanding Tables

What You Will Learn

In this lesson, you look at tables, which are the foundation of relational databases. Understanding how data is stored in tables and the basics of normalization can provide a solid base for looking at relational databases.

We Will Cover

- What tables are

- How records are stored in rows

- How attributes or records are stored in columns

- System data types

- User-defined data types

- Primary keys

Notes from the Lesson

- Tables store all data in SQL Server databases.

- Each record or row in a table should only contain data that pertains to one instance of an object. For example, in an employee table, all the data in a single row will pertain to a single employee.

- Data types define the sort of information that can be stored in a column. For example, an `int` data type means that only integer data can be stored in that column.

- A primary key is the column or columns that can uniquely identify a specific record in a table.

lesson ⊙ 8

Understanding Relationships

What You Will Learn

In this lesson, you look at relationships between tables. This is where you start to understand the power of relational databases. Without relationships, you could just use Excel spreadsheets instead of databases. We look at all the types of relationships you might encounter and talk a little more about normalization.

We Will Cover

- Foreign keys
- One-to-many relationships
- One-to-one relationships
- Many-to-many relationships

Notes from the Lesson

- Relationships allow you to tie data in multiple tables together.
- Foreign keys are the links from one table to the primary key of another table; they are the physical implementation of relationships.
- One-to-many or 1:M relationships relate one row in a table to one or more rows in another table.
- One-to-one or 1:1 relationships relate one row in a table to one and only one row in another table.
- Many-to-many or M:M relationships relate many rows in one table to many rows in another table. This is actually accomplished by using a junction table that has a 1:M relationship to each of the tables involved in the M:M relationship.

lesson ⊙ 9

Database Files

What You Will Learn

You take your first good look at how SQL Server manages databases. You look at the types of files that make up databases and how to use them. You also look at file groups, an important concept for managing files. In SSMS, files are managed in the database Properties dialog box, as shown in Figure 9.1. You can also administer everything about files using Transact SQL.

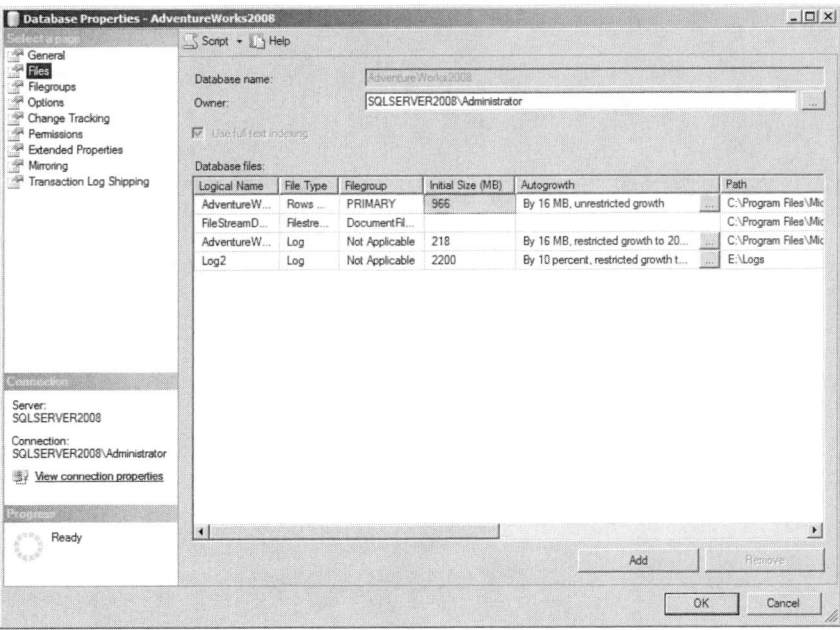

Figure 9.1   Managing data files in SQL Server Management Studio.

We Will Cover

- Data files

- Transaction log files

- Filestream data files

- File groups

Notes from the Lesson

- Data files contain all the data in a database. Indexes are also stored in data files.

- The transaction log consists of one or more log files. Log files cannot be grouped, and all the log files work together to form the Transaction Log.

- For storing filestream data new to SQL Server 2008, filestream data files are used.

- File groups allow you to separate data files into groups to optimize I/O reads-and-writes. Take great care when grouping data files and make sure you test your solutions. Incorrect use of file groups can degrade performance.

lesson ⊙ 10

The Transaction Log

What You Will Learn

The Transaction Log is vital to the operation of SQL Server databases. Knowing what it is, how it works, and where to go to change its settings will be invaluable knowledge for you while working with SQL Server. In this lesson, you lay the groundwork for the Transaction Log so that you can better understand it.

We Will Cover

- How the Transaction Log works
- Understanding checkpoints
- Database recovery models

Notes from the Lesson

- The Transaction Log records all transactions that run against a SQL Server before they are written to the database.
- When checkpoints occur, committed transactions are written to the database.
- The three recovery models available on databases are simple, full, and bulk-logged.

lesson ⊙ 11

Understanding System Databases

What You Will Learn

System databases control the operation of SQL Server. They are a similar to user databases except that the data in them apply to the entire server, and damage to them can cause the server to fail. In this lesson, we look at each of the system databases and discuss the type of information they each hold. When applicable, we look at how some system databases differ from user databases.

We Will Cover

- Master database
- Model database
- MSDB
- TempDB
- Distribution database

Notes from the Lesson

- The master database contains all the information about the other databases, as well as server-level information such as configuration and security. Anytime you make changes to the server that isn't specific to another database, you should make sure that you back up the master database. This includes adding a new database to the server.

- Model is simply a template for new databases. All the database settings, including size, recovery model, and compatibility level, will be inherited by any new user database created on the server. You shouldn't need to back up this database unless you make significant changes to the settings and you don't want to reapply the settings if you lose the database.

- The MSDB database is the job-and-alerting database in SQL Server. All options related to jobs, alerts, operators, and so on would be stored in MSDB. Make sure you back up every time you change one of these objects that is handled by MSDB.

- TempDB is a database that SQL Server uses whenever it needs temporary space to perform a query. Because all the information is temporary and TempDB is cleared out each time the server restarts, there is no need to back up this database.

- The distributor in a replication topology uses the distribution database. This database will only be present if replication is enabled and the server is a distributor.

lesson ⊙ 12

Processor Settings

What You Will Learn

In this brief lesson, you look at the processor settings for SQL Server. These settings allow you to control how SQL Server works with CPUs, especially on a multiprocessor system.

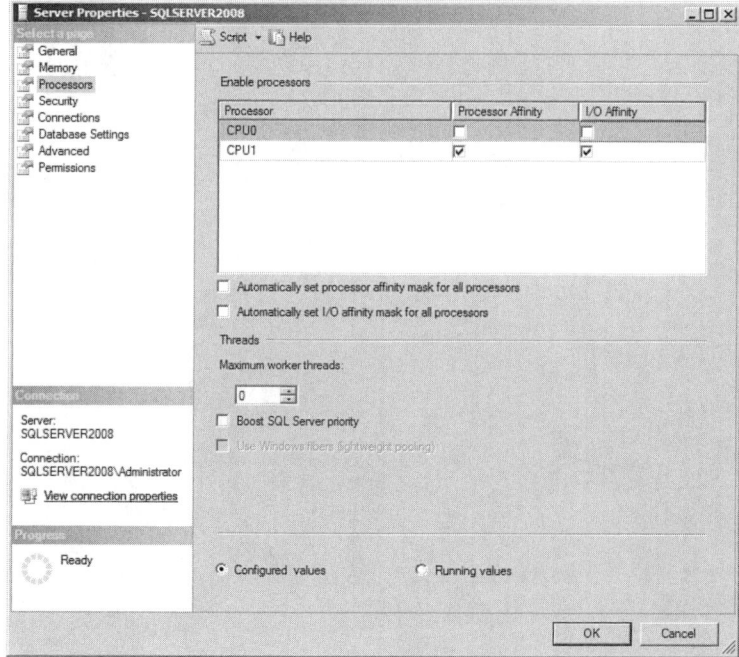

Figure 12.1   The processor settings for an instance of SQL Server.

We Will Cover

- Working with multiple processors

- Understanding processor options

Notes from the Lesson

- You can limit SQL Server to work with fewer processors than exist in the system. This is useful if you have multiple instances and you don't want any one instance using all the resources.

- You can also set advanced options such as Maximum Worker Threads, or you can choose to boost the SQL Server priority.

- Make sure you do your homework before changing these settings; incorrect configurations can greatly degrade your server's performance.

lesson⊙ 13

Memory Settings

What You Will Learn

In yet another brief lesson, you look at the memory settings for SQL Server. Using these options, you can limit the amount of physical memory SQL Server uses for general operations, index creation, or even individual queries. In addition, depending on the configuration of your server, you might need to tweak these settings to make use of all available memory.

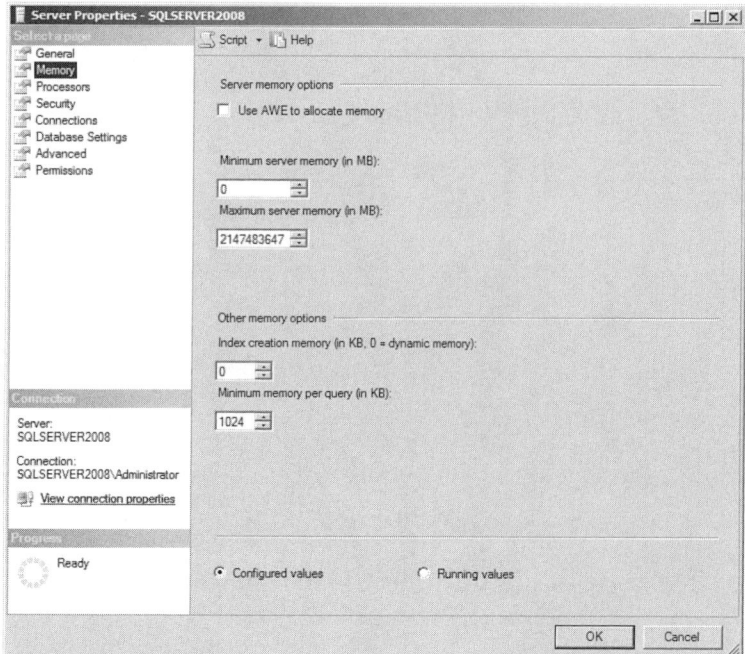

Figure 13.1   The memory settings for an instance of SQL Server.

We Will Cover

- Configuring SQL Server memory options

- Limiting SQL Server memory usage

- AWE memory options

Notes from the Lesson

- You can limit both the minimum and maximum amount of memory you want SQL Server to use. By default, SQL Server uses as much or as little as needed.

- You can also limit the amount of memory that SQL Server uses for index creation. This is a good option if you are less concerned with index creation time and more concerned with the availability of memory resources for other tasks.

- You might need to enable the AWE Memory option to access all the memory on your server. This setting behaves differently depending on the operating system. Be sure you research your specific environment before enabling this option. Also, note that on 64-bit systems, this option is not needed and cannot be configured.

lesson ⊙ 14

Backing Up Databases

What You Will Learn

One of the most important things you can do with your SQL Servers is to back up the databases. If a server fails because of corrupt data, your backup might be the only thing that saves you from losing data. In this lesson, you look at the different backup types and how to perform them. We cover backing up from SSMS, as shown in Figure 14.1, and how to back up using T-SQL.

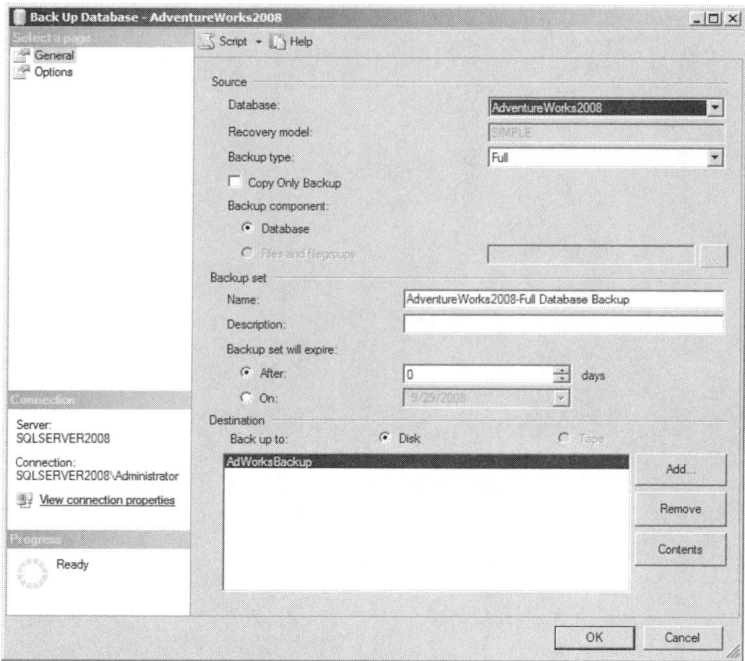

Figure 14.1   The GUI for performing backups in SSMS.

We Will Cover

- Backup types
- Performing backups

Notes from the Lesson

- The three different backup types are Full backups, Differential backups, and Transaction Log backups.

- Full backups back up all the data in a given database.

- Differential backups back up all data that has changed since the last full backup.

- Transaction Log backups back up all the data in the transaction log. After the data is backed up, it is written to the database, thus freeing space in the Transaction Log. You cannot perform this backup on databases using the Simple Recovery model.

lesson ⊙ 15

Scheduling Backups

What You Will Learn

Now that you understand how to run backups on your SQL Server databases, you probably don't want to run them manually 10 times a day. In this lesson, you look at how to use SQL Server Agent jobs to schedule the running of your backups. This lesson also serves as a great introduction to jobs in general so that you can eventfully schedule all your maintenance jobs to run automatically.

We Will Cover
- Using SQL Server jobs
- Using maintenance plans

Notes from the Lesson
- You can use SQL Server jobs to run processes on a regular basis. You can run T-SQL, PowerShell, ActiveX scripts, batch files, and several other SQL Server processes using jobs.
- Full Schedules control when and how often jobs will run.
- You can also configure maintenance plans to run common SQL Server maintenance tasks. Maintenance plans can be set up with a simple wizard or built using a designer for more flexibility and power.

lesson ⊙ 16

Restoring Databases

What You Will Learn

What good are backups if you can't use those backups to re-create your databases when the need arises? Restoring databases in SQL Server is straightforward, but just as with backups, you must become familiar with a few nuances. In this lesson, we run through the ins and outs of restoring databases and make sure that you know what to expect when restoring.

We Will Cover

- Restore types
- Restoring using the SSMS

Notes from the Lesson

- The three types of restores match the backup types you looked at in the previous lesson. Full, Differential, and Transaction Log restores are done from the corresponding backup types.
- The order in which you restore your backups is crucial. You must restore the most recent Full, followed by the most recent Differential, if you have one, and then followed by an unbroken chain of Transaction Log backups that were taken after the last Differential or Full backup.

lesson ⊙ 17

Restoring System Databases

What You Will Learn

Systems databases are a little different in terms of how you handle restores. Because they are required for the operation of SQL Server, you can't just overwrite them without first taking a few other steps. This lesson looks at each system database and covers what you need to know to restore them successfully.

We Will Cover

- Restoring MSDB
- Restoring Model
- Restoring Master

Notes from the Lesson

- Restore MSDB like you restore a user database. The only caveat is that you must shut down SQL Server Agent before you can restore.

- Model is restored like a user database.

- Master is the trickiest system database to restore. The SQL Server needs to be started in single-user mode. This is done by stopping the SQL Server service, adding the –m startup option using Configuration Manager, as shown in Figure 17.1, and then restarting the SQL Server Service.

Figure 17.1   Setting the single user startup parameter in Configuration
Manager.

lesson ⊙ 18

Managing Logins

What You Will Learn

Your first level of security in SQL Server is the login. Logins define who can access your SQL Server. Without a login, users cannot connect to your SQL Server—or to the databases and objects defined on the server. This lesson looks at logins, authentication modes, and the types of permissions that you can assign to logins.

We Will Cover

- Authentication mode
- Windows logins
- SQL Server logins
- Assigning permissions

Notes from the Lesson

- SQL Server has two authentication modes: Windows Authentication and SQL Server Authentication.
- Windows Authentication mode allows you to define logins that map to existing Windows users or groups. This method allows users to be authenticated by Windows or Active Directory before access is granted to the SQL Server.
- With SQL Server Authentication mode, logins and passwords are stored on your SQL Server, and all authentication is handled by SQL Server. This is appropriate when you are not in a Windows environment or in other situations when Windows Authentication might not be possible, such as a user on a UNIX client or in a DMZ.

lesson ⏵ 19

Managing Users

What You Will Learn

After you set up logins on the SQL Server, you need to create users. Users constitute your second line of security because they permit access into individual databases. All user accounts are linked to logins, so your end users generally don't need to worry about anything other than their login credentials.

We Will Cover

- Creating users
- Linking to logins

Notes from the Lesson

- All database users must be related to a login, or they will be orphaned.
- You can assign permissions directly to users, but it is often better to use database roles, which we look at in Lesson 20.

lesson ⊙ 20

Database Roles

What You Will Learn

Database roles are like groups of users. Creating roles and assigning permissions to the roles will give all users in the role that permission. This is often the best way to handle permissions because you won't need to assign permissions to individual users. Unlike server roles, you can create your own database roles to manage your environment and requirements.

We Will Cover

- Using database roles
- Creating database roles

Notes from the Lesson

- Database roles are created in the Database Roles folder under an individual database, as shown in Figure 20.1
- You can assign permissions directly to users, but it is often better to use database roles.

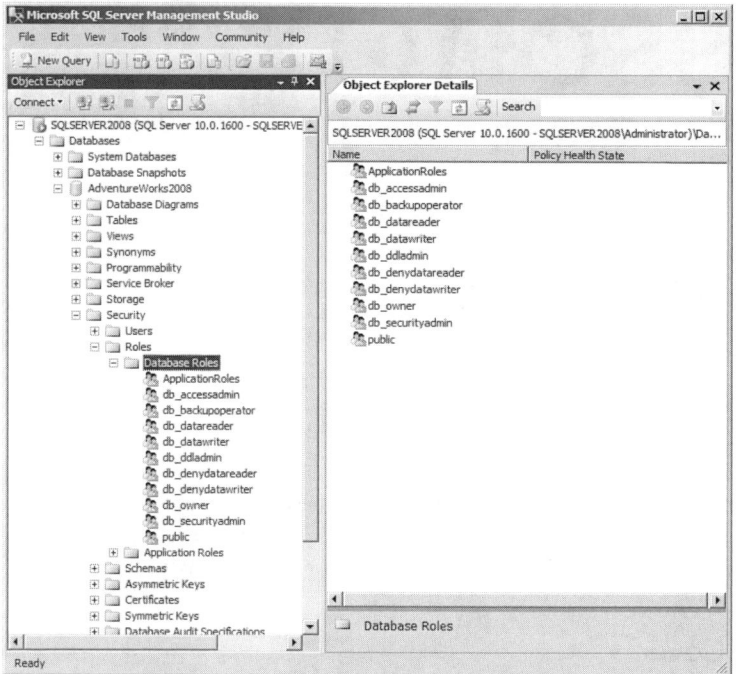

Figure 20.1   The Database Roles folder in SSMS.

lesson ⊙ 21

Ownership Chaining

What You Will Learn

SQL Server allows permissions assigned to one object to be transferred to another object if the owner of each of these objects is the same. This is known as ownership chaining. It allows you to write a procedure that references a table without the need to assign permissions for a user to read the table. If the user can execute the procedure and the table has the same owner as the procedure, you will be good to go.

We Will Cover

- Understanding ownership chaining
- How Dynamic SQL works with ownership chaining

Notes from the Lesson

- The owners of each object in the chain must be the same.
- You can set up cross database ownership chaining on individual databases.
- If you reference an object with dynamic SQL inside a stored procedure, ownership chaining will not work, even if the owners are the same.

lesson ⏵ 22

Data Manipulation Language

What You Will Learn

Transact SQL, or T-SQL, is Microsoft's implementation of Structure Query Language that is defined by the ANSI-92 standard. T-SQL is a programming language of sorts that you use to manipulate data and objects in databases. We are not going to get too deep into T-SQL in this LiveLesson, but you do need a fundamental understanding of it to administer SQL Server. In this lesson, we look at Data Manipulation Language (DML), which is the T-SQL syntax that you use to view and change data. There is far more to DML than what we cover here, but everything stems from the statements we review.

We Will Cover

- INSERT statement

- UPDATE statement

- DELETE statement

- SELECT statement

Notes from the Lesson

- The SELECT statement will probably be the one you spend the most time working with and is also the statement with the most options.

- To filter a SELECT, UPDATE, or DELETE statement, use a WHERE clause.

- INSERT allows you to add new records to a table.

- Use UPDATE to change the values of existing data in existing records.

- Use the DELETE statement to remove records from a table.

lesson ⏵ 23

Data Definition Language

What You Will Learn

In this lesson, we continue our discussion of T-SQL by looking at Data Definition Language (DDL), which is the syntax that allows you to create and modify database objects, such as views, tables, and stored procedures. Depending on the objects you work with, the syntax will be slightly different, but most DDL falls into three major statement types: CREATE, ALTER, and DROP.

We Will Cover

- CREATE statement

- ALTER statement

- DROP statement

Notes from the Lesson

- To make new objects in SQL Server, use a CREATE statement. For example, to create a simple stored procedure, use the following code:

```
CREATE PROCEDURE HelloWorld
AS
PRINT 'Hello World'
```

- Objects are modified by using the ALTER statement. To add a new column called ssn to the existing Employee table, use this code:

```
ALTER TABLE Employee
ADD ssn varchar(25)
```

- Use the DROP statement to delete objects from the database. For example, to drop the HelloWorld stored procedure, use the following code:

```
DROP PROCEDURE HelloWorld
```

lesson ⊙ 24

Stored Procedures

What You Will Learn

SQL Server uses stored procedures to store bits of T-SQL code that can be called like a module in a programming language. You can run any piece of T-SQL code to manipulate the data or objects in the database or to select data from the database. It is always a good practice for applications that access SQL Server databases to do so via stored procedures, rather than T-SQL embedded in applications. We talk more about that in Lesson 33 when we look at abstraction layers, but for now let's look at exactly what stored procedures are and how you work with them.

We Will Cover

- Understanding stored procedures

- Creating stored procedures

- Working with stored procedure security

Notes from the Lesson

- Stored procedures are compiled bits or T-SQL.

- Most everything you can do in T-SQL can be placed into a stored procedure.

- Create stored procedures by using the CREATE PROCEDURE DDL statement as shown here.

  ```
  CREATE PROCEDURE HelloWorld
  AS
  PRINT 'HelloWorld'
  ```

- The most frequent permission you will assign on stored procedure will be the permission to EXECUTE the procedure.

lesson ▶ 25

Functions

What You Will Learn

Functions are similar to stored procedures in that they contain chunks or T-SQL code. The major difference is that you cannot modify objects with code in functions. They are meant to return data as either single scalar values or tables. If you need to modify data, you need to use a combination of functions and stored procedures that can be called by functions. The other big difference with functions is that they can be called in line with other code. In fact, they behave just like the built-in SQL Server functions.

We Will Cover

- Understanding functions

- Creating functions

- Working with function security

Notes from the Lesson

- Functions are used to retrieve data; you cannot modify objects in a function.

- When creating functions, you must specify the type of data that the function is to return.

- Create functions by using the CREATE FUNCTION DDL statement as shown here.

```
CREATE FUNCTION GetCustomerAddress (@customerid int)
RETURNS int
AS
BEGIN
DECLARE @addressid int
SELECT addressid  = AddressID FROM Customer
WHERE customerid = @customerid
RETURN addressid
END
```

- The most frequent permission you will assign on functions will be the permission to EXECUTE.

lesson ⊙ 26

Views

What You Will Learn

Views are stored SELECT statements that return data from one or more underlying tables. When you select data from a view, it comes back just as though you had selected data from a table. Views are preferred to going directly to tables for several reasons, one being security. We will look closely at this is Lesson 33 when we discuss abstraction layers.

We Will Cover

- Understanding views
- Creating views
- Working with view security

Notes from the Lesson

- Use views to retrieve data from one or more tables by using SELECT statements.
- Create views by using the CREATE VIEW DDL statement as shown here.

```
CREATE VIEW ActiveEmployees
AS
SELECT * FROM Employee
WHERE active = 1
```

- The permissions you assign on views are similar to those you set on tables. Most commonly, you grant users the permission to INSERT, UPDATE, SELECT, or DELETE from views. You can also grant permissions to ALTER or VIEW DEFINITION that allows users to see the code that comprises the view.

lesson ⊙ 27

Triggers

What You Will Learn

Triggers are similar to stored procedures in that they store T-SQL code for later execution. The difference is that they cannot be called by a user or application. Instead they are linked to tables or views and set up to run when a DML statement is run against the table or view to which the trigger is linked. Triggers allow you to have special code run in response to an INSERT, UPDATE, or DELETE statement.

We Will Cover

- Understanding triggers
- Creating triggers

Notes from the Lesson

- Triggers can be linked to INSERT, UPDATE, DELETE, or a combination of these statements. When the DML statement is specified in a run, the trigger will fire running its own code.

- Triggers come in two styles: INSTEAD OF triggers that run their code instead of the original code executed against the object, and AFTER triggers that run their code after the DML statement that fired the trigger.

- Code in triggers can access two special tables, INSERTED and DELETED. This allows triggers to see the data as it existed before and after the triggering DML statement.

- Create triggers by using the CREATE TRIGGER DDL statement as shown here.

```
CREATE TRIGGER UpdateLog
ON Customer
AFTER INSERT, UPDATE
AS
EXEC UpdateCustomerLog
GO
```

lesson ⊙ 28

CLR Integration

What You Will Learn

SQL Server 2005 was the first version of SQL Server to introduce CLR Integration. You can write code in a CLR-based language such as VB.NET or C# and then link that code to an object in SQL Server, such as a function or stored procedure. This gives you the flexibility to use the power of CLR code in your SQL Server environment. The best part is that all the other objects in your databases can reference these CLR objects as though they were regular SQL Server procedures and functions.

We Will Cover

- Understanding CLR Integration
- Creating CLR procedures
- Creating CLR functions

Notes from the Lesson

- Your CLR code must be written in a separate program such as Visual Studio. Code is then imported as assemblies, and functions or procedures are created based on modules in the assembly.
- The three code access security levels for managed CLR Code running on SQL Server are SAFE, EXTERNAL_ACCESS, and UNSAFE.
- SAFE code is allowed to access only local data and perform computations.
- EXTERNAL_ACCESS allows code to also access objects on the OS, such as files and the Registry.
- The UNSAFE security mode has unrestricted access to resources inside and outside of SQL Server and can call unmanaged code.

lesson ⊙ 29

Indexing Overview

What You Will Learn

Managing SQL Server indexing is one of the most important things that a SQL Server DBA needs to do. It can also be one of the most challenging and is often referred to as a black art. Indexes help SQL Server to locate data in a database much like a book index helps you find information in a book. Too many or too few indexes have the potential to cause performance problems on your server. Indexes need to be just like the baby bear's porridge—just right.

We Will Cover

- How indexes work
- How indexes are implemented

Notes from the Lesson

- Indexes are meant to speed up the reading of data, but they will slow down write operations.
- Fillfactor determines how full each page will get before writing to another page. For example, filling a page to 80% leaves room in the page to add new data to the index as needed, which prevents the index from become fragmented.

lesson ⊙ 30

Working with Indexes

What You Will Learn

Indexes come in two flavors: clustered and nonclustered. Clustered indexes are stored with the data and in order. Nonclustered indexes are stored separately from the data and used more like a reference to locate data. In this lesson, we look at creating indexes in SQL Server; both clustered and nonclustered indexes will be covered.

We Will Cover

- Clustered indexes

- Nonclustered indexes

Notes from the Lesson

- Nonclustered indexes are the most like a traditional book index. They are stored separately, and you use them as references to find data in the table.

- Clustered indexes are stored with the data and are more like dictionaries. The index is the data and the data is the index; when you find the word you are looking for, the "data" or definition is right there.

lesson ⊙ 31

Included Columns

What You Will Learn

Indexes can also contain included columns. This allows you to have data that is part of the index stored in the same pages of the index. This can lead to faster data retrieval because the process does not have to traverse from the index to the data page to get the values you are looking for. In this lesson we look at how you can add included columns to indexes.

We Will Cover

- Understanding included columns
- Using included columns

Notes from the Lesson

- Data in included columns is physically stored with the index in which it is included.
- Although included columns can be a great time-saver, overuse can lead to large index sizes and slower write performance.

lesson ⦿ 32

Application Security

What You Will Learn

When working with security for applications that will be accessing your SQL Server, you have several options. There is some debate over which model is better, and I am not endorsing any specific one here. Regardless of whether you use SQL Server Logins or Windows Authentication, you still have to decide whether an application will use a single login to access SQL Server (and all appropriate database objects) or allow each individual user to have his own login. Each model has its own sets of pros and cons, but I want to focus on a specific con of each user having his own login. The biggest issue is that each user login has access to your server and to one or more databases. Does the user need to delete data as part of his job? If so, he will have this right whether he logs in via an application or directly to the server. Often, the application controls what can and cannot be deleted based on a set of business rules; these rules usually don't exist on the SQL Server itself. In short, if each user has his own login, he can access SQL Server directly and potentially cause some damage.

We Will Cover

- Setting up a single application login
- Using one login for each user
- Application roles

lesson ⊙ 33

Abstraction Layers

What You Will Learn

Abstraction layers are important aspects of database systems. A correctly configured abstraction layer provides security and shields users and applications for change that might occur to underlying tables.

We Will Cover

- Setting up abstraction layers
- Benefits of abstraction layers

Notes from the Lesson

- Most commonly, you use views or functions to provide read-access to data and stored procedures to modify data.

- Abstraction layers prevent users and applications from being affected by changes to the database structure if the abstraction layer is updated to reflect the changes.

- You lessen your security risk by not giving users and applications direct access to the tables and also reduce the risk of exposing new data accidentally.